PIANO ACCOMPANIMENT

PATRIOTIC FAVORITES

Solos and Band Arrangements
Correlated with Essential Elements Band Method

Arranged by
MICHAEL SWEENEY

Welcome to Essential Elements Patriotic Favorites! The arrangements in this versatile book can be used either in a full concert band setting or as solos for individual instruments. The SOLO pages appear at the beginning of the book, followed by the BAND ARRANGEMENT pages. The supplemental CD recording or PIANO ACCOMPANIMENT book may be used as an accompaniment for solo performance.

ISBN 0-634-05029-X

HAL•LEONARD®
CORPORATION

7777 W. BLUEMOUND RD. P.O. BOX 13819 MILWAUKEE, WI 53213

AMERICA, THE BEAUTIFUL

Words by KATHERINE LEE BATES
Music by SAMUEL A. WARD
Arranged by MICHAEL SWEENEY

00860103

BATTLE HYMN OF THE REPUBLIC

Words by JULIA WARD HOWE
Music by WILLIAM STEFFE
Arranged by MICHAEL SWEENEY

00860103

GOD BLESS AMERICA®

Words and Music by
IRVING BERLIN
Arranged by MICHAEL SWEENEY

00860103

MY COUNTRY, 'TIS OF THEE
(America)

Words by SAMUEL FRANCIS SMITH
Music from THESAURUS MUSICUS
Arranged by MICHAEL SWEENEY

THIS IS MY COUNTRY

Words by DON RAYE
Music by AL JACOBS
Arranged by MICHAEL SWEENEY

00860103

16

00860103

From the Paramount and DreamWorks Motion Picture SAVING PRIVATE RYAN

HYMN TO THE FALLEN

Music by JOHN WILLIAMS
Arranged by MICHAEL SWEENEY

00860103

18

00860103

YANKEE DOODLE/YANKEE DOODLE BOY

Traditional
Arranged by MICHAEL SWEENEY

From the Motion Picture THE PATRIOT

THE PATRIOT

Composed by JOHN WILLIAMS
Arranged by MICHAEL SWEENEY

ARMED FORCES SALUTE

Arranged by MICHAEL SWEENEY

MARINE'S HYMN
Words by HENRY C. DAVIS
Melody based on a theme by JACQUES OFFENBACH
Copyright © 2002 by HAL LEONARD CORPORATION
International Copyright Secured   All Rights Reserved

THE CAISSONS GO ROLLING ALONG
Words and Music by EDMUND L. GRUBER
Copyright © 2002 by HAL LEONARD CORPORATION
International Copyright Secured   All Rights Reserved

ANCHORS AWEIGH
Words by ALFRED HART MILES and ROYAL LOVELL
Music by CHARLES A. ZIMMERMAN
Additional Lyric by GEORGE D. LOTTMAN
Copyright © 2002 by HAL LEONARD CORPORATION
International Copyright Secured   All Rights Reserved

STARS AND STRIPES FOREVER

By JOHN PHILIP SOUSA
Arranged by MICHAEL SWEENEY

THE STAR SPANGLED BANNER

Words by FRANCIS SCOTT KEY
Music by JOHN STAFFORD SMITH
Arranged by MICHAEL SWEENEY

MORE
FAVORITES FROM
ESSENTIAL ELEMENTS

These superb collections feature favorite songs that students can play as they progress through their band method books. Each song is arranged to be played by either a full band or by individual soloists, with optional accompaniment on CD.

Each song appears twice in the book, featuring:
- Solo instrument version
- Band arrangement for full band or ensembles
- Pop-style accompaniment CD included with conductor's score
- Accompaniment CD available separately
- Piano accompaniment book that is compatible with recorded backgrounds

Prices:
- Conductor Books $24.99
- Instrument Books $6.99
- Piano Accompaniment Books $11.99
- Accompaniment CDs. $12.99

Instrument books for each collection feature separate books for the following: Flute, Oboe, Bassoon, B♭ Clarinet, E♭ Alto Clarinet, B♭ Bass Clarinet, E♭ Alto Saxophone, B♭ Tenor Saxophone, E♭ Baritone Saxophone, B♭ Trumpet, F Horn, Trombone, Baritone B.C., Baritone T.C., Tuba, Percussion, and Keyboard Percussion.

BROADWAY FAVORITES
Arranged by Michael Sweeney
Songs include:
Beauty and the Beast
Tomorrow
Cabaret
Edelweiss
Don't Cry for Me Argentina
Get Me to the Church on Time
I Dreamed a Dream
Go Go Go Joseph
Memory
The Phantom of the Opera
Seventy Six Trombones

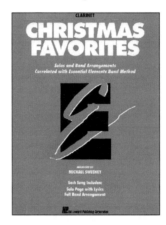

CHRISTMAS FAVORITES
Arranged by Michael Sweeney
Songs include:
The Christmas Song
 (Chestnuts Roasting on an Open Fire)
Frosty the Snow Man
A Holly Jolly Christmas
Jingle-Bell Rock
Let It Snow! Let It Snow! Let It Snow!
Rockin' Around the Christmas Tree
Rudolph, the Red-Nosed Reindeer.

FILM FAVORITES
Arranged by Michael Sweeney, John Moss and Paul Lavender
Songs include:
The Black Pearl
Fairytale Opening
Mission: Impossible Theme
My Heart Will Go On
Zorro's Theme
Music from Shrek
May It Be
The Medallion Calls
You'll Be in My Heart
The Rainbow Connection
Accidentally in Love
Also Sprach Zarathustra

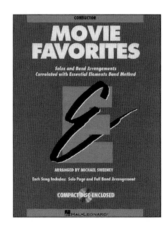

MOVIE FAVORITES
Arranged by Michael Sweeney
Includes themes from:
An American Tail
Back to the Future
Chariots of Fire
Apollo 13
E.T.
Forrest Gump
Dances with Wolves
Jurassic Park
The Man from Snowy River
Raiders of the Lost Ark
Star Trek

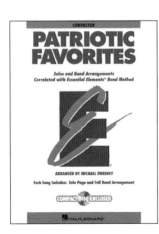

PATRIOTIC FAVORITES
Arranged by Michael Sweeney
Songs include:
America, the Beautiful
Armed Forces Salute
Battle Hymn of the Republic
God Bless America
Hymn to the Fallen
My Country, 'Tis of Thee (America)
The Patriot
The Star Spangled Banner
Stars and Stripes Forever
This Is My Country
Yankee Doodle/Yankee Dookle Boy

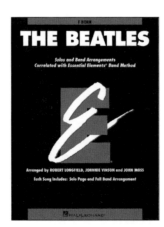

THE BEATLES
Arranged by Robert Longfield, Johnnie Vinson and John Moss
Songs include:
And I Love Her
A Hard Day's Night
Yesterday
Get Back
Lady Madonna
Twist and Shout
Hey Jude
Eleanor Rigby
Ticket to Ride
Here, There and Everywhere
I Want to Hold Your Hand

HAL•LEONARD®
Visit Hal Leonard Online at **www.halleonard.com**